FAITHFUL TO THE END

A 40-DAY DEVOTIONAL

HOPE BEALE PH.D.

WHITE RAIMENT PUBLICATION

Copyright © 2021 by Hope Beale, Ph.D.

All rights reserved.

No part of this book may be reproduced in any form or by any electronic or mechanical means, including information storage and retrieval systems, without written permission from the author, except for the use of brief quotations in a book review.

Subject Heading: Salvation, Grace, Faith, Faithfulness, Trust, Truth, Devotional

Scripture quotations are from The Holy Bible, King James Version, Public Domain

Published by White Raiment Publication

For more information, please contact White Raiment Publication at hope@wr7publication.com

Disclaimer:

Faithful to the End is not intended to diagnose or treat your individual concerns. All information provided in this book is for educational purposes only and does not constitute a one-on-one therapeutic, medical or legal relationship, nor does it replace counseling from a pastor, physician, attorney, or therapist. If at any time you feel that you need advice, please contact your local health care professional.

DEDICATION

To the faint at heart, the tired, anxious, fearful, discouraged, and disappointed, our Heavenly Father hasn't forgotten… He will give you His strength and courage to be faithful to the end.

We know not the precise time when our Lord shall be revealed in the clouds of heaven; but He has told us that our only safety is in a constant readiness,—a position of watching and waiting. Whether we have one year before us, or five, or ten, we are to be faithful to our trust today. We are to perform each day's duties as faithfully as though that day were to be our last.

Ellen White, *Signs of the Times,* April 14, 1887, par. 4

CONTENTS

Faithful	xi
About the Author	xv
The Grace to be Authentic	1
Introduction	3
1. Our need of God	9
2. Everlasting arm of Jesus	11
3. Courage	14
4. God is in control	15
5. A heart of gratitude	18
6. The strength of the Almighty	23
7. A friend in Jesus	25
8. Our Redeemer lives	28
9. God meets all our needs	30
10. Mighty Confidence	33
11. Jesus's victorious life	38
12. God's faithfulness	40
13. God's love	43
14. Not forsaken of God	45
15. Fearless	47
16. Quietness and confident	51
17. Christ's victorious life	53
18. All Controls	56
19. When we are afraid	58
20. Total reliance	61
21. Prince of Peace	65
22. Peace of God	66
23. Fearlessly loved	69
24. Glorified Redeemer	71
25. Strength of the Lord	74
26. The yoke of Christ	79
27. The goodness of the Lord	81

28. Transforming power of God	84
29. Light of Christ's love, mercy, and grace	86
30. Quiet peace	89
31. Safe place	93
32. The power of brokenness	95
33. Constant	98
34. First believed	99
35. God's courage	101
36. God's mercy	105
37. Rejoicing	107
38. God's mind	110
39. God is big enough	112
40. Even This…	115

Faithful to the End:
A 40-Day Devotional

Cause me to hear Thy lovingkindness *in the morning*; for in Thee do I trust: cause me to know the way wherein I should walk; for I lift up my soul unto Thee. Psalm 143:8

FAITHFUL

One of my favorite stories in the Bible is that of Joseph, Israel's son. It is a story of privilege, love, family, promises. It is also a story of hate, indulgence, anger, cruel deeds, separation, revenge, and deception,

I've thought a lot about Joseph and how God fulfills His plan through him. Long before his birth, God would raise up a nation to represent Him, and Joseph was part of that plan. But God had to prepare Joseph to be a vehicle He could use. (Read Genesis 37, 39)

After his brothers sold him to a caravan journeying to Egypt, he knew not what his future would be. He was alone, confused, and afraid. He did not have his earthy father to turn to; then, he remembered his father's God.

As part of this devotional, I want to give you a backdrop to my pursuit to be faithful to God; therefore, I am including a small section of Joseph's story that illustrates his determination to prove himself faithful to God. The excerpt you will read helped put things in perspective when I needed to understand what it meant to be faithful to the Lord. It was written by Ellen White and taken from her book title *Patriarchs and Prophets*, pages 213-14.

When faced with difficulties and an uncertain future, remember that God, who met Joseph on the way to Egypt, will meet us in our journey.

∼

Jospeh in Egypt
by Ellen White

But, in the providence of God, even this experience was to be a blessing to him. He had learned in a few hours that which years might not otherwise have taught him. His father, strong and tender as his love had been, had done him wrong by his partiality and indulgence. This unwise preference had angered his brothers and provoked them to the cruel deed that had separated him from his home. Its effects were manifest also in his own character. Faults had been encouraged that were now to be corrected. He was becoming self-sufficient and exacting. Accustomed to the tenderness of his father's care, he felt that he was unprepared to cope with the difficulties before him, in the bitter, uncared-for life of a stranger and a slave.

Then his thoughts turned to his father's God. In his childhood he had been taught to love and fear Him. Often in his father's tent he had listened to the story of the vision that Jacob saw as he fled from his home an exile and a fugitive. He had been told of the Lord's promises to Jacob, and how they had been fulfilled—how, in the hour of need, the angels of God had come to instruct, comfort, and protect him. And he had learned of the love of God in providing for men a Redeemer.

Now all these precious lessons came vividly before him. Joseph believed that the God of his fathers would be his God. He then and there gave himself fully to the Lord, and he prayed that the Keeper of Israel would be with him in the land of his exile.

His soul thrilled with the high resolve to prove himself true to God—under all circumstances to act as became a subject of the King of heaven. He would serve the Lord with undivided heart; he would meet the trials of his lot with fortitude and perform every duty with fidelity. One day's experience had been the turning point in Joseph's life. Its terrible calamity had transformed him from a petted child to a man, thoughtful, courageous, and self-possessed.

What a powerful testimony!

Joseph's resolve to prove himself faithful to God thrilled and frighten me. I wondered if I had what it took to take such a journey. Then I remembered whose strength, grace and love Joseph rested in. My faith was renewed. My confidence restored.

I believe it was a daily decision that Joseph made to serve God with an undivided heart. I believe there were days he made that decision several times a day. It couldn't have been easy and at times it must have been very hard… Read the rest of Joseph's story and you will discover that for several years his decision to be faithful to God was tested and tested and tested.

I've often imagined the conversations Joseph had with the Lord, "Father, get me through one more day…" "I don't know if I can do this…"

After much time in prayer, soul searching, and surrendering his heart and circumstances to God, Joseph is ready to show himself faithful to God one more time. May this be our greatest desire.

ABOUT THE AUTHOR

On July 20, 2009, I was officially diagnosed with a learning disability. I say officially because several years prior, the Lord shared with me that I had dyslexia. I also learned that I was not alone. Millions of people, young and old, have some form of dyslexia, which is a neurological disorder that affects a person's ability to learn how to read, write, and spell. It is an inherited disorder, and unless God intervenes, it doesn't go away. I will have dyslexia for the rest of my life. As with any disability or disorder, a person will fall somewhere on a continuum ranging from mild to profound.

The good news is that children, teens, and adults can learn to read, write, and advance in school due in part to the advancement of research. What is not often openly discussed is the emotional trauma and spiritual impact having a disability may have on a person (e.g., feeling defeated, hopelessness, learned helplessness, low-self-worth, isolation).

God's Sufficiency

I am thankful that God encouraged me to pursue His dream, which included earning a doctoral degree. It was tough and there were days I wondered if I would be able to reach this goal. However, in 2016 I was awarded a doctorate in Psychology with a specialization in Educational Psychology.

The greatest lesson I learned is that God's grace is sufficient; it is more than enough, even for healing my wounded heart from the emotional impact of having a disability (2 Corinthians 12:9). I also believe that each person that has a disability is uniquely gifted by God to take part in His work. This is why I believe God has a sense of humor that His purpose for me would include writing and speaking on His behalf. Remember, I have dyslexia; however, this has never been a deterrent for the Lord. All He requires is a willing, trusting heart that I daily surrendered my dyslexia and its emotional impact to Him (Isaiah 55:11).

The Beginning

My writing started when I began to keep journals. This was an outlet for me to put down on paper my daily struggles with life. Then I noticed when I would read something from God's word or hear something in a song that encouraged or challenged me, I knew I had to capture it in some way that I could pass it along to someone else. My first venture of seriously writing came in the form of creating greeting cards. I never published them, but I still have them and plan to do so.

Then I became interested in writing a book. I laugh now because back then, self-publishing was not very popular, and I didn't think anyone would be that interested in what I had to say. I certainly didn't think I could compete with those famous authors. Yet, I found myself writing and writing. I can't tell you how many books I have started that I never finished. At some point, I think I gave up on writing and publishing a book and poured myself into creating websites. I figured if I never published a book, my websites would be a vehicle that I could write for God. Those websites never took off... The desire to put my story, journey with dyslexia, never left me, and this went on for ten years.

The Grace to be Authentic

One day while expressing my frustration to the Lord, I knew I could not put it off any longer. Self-publishing was the new kid on the block. Everyone seems to be going in that direction, which gave me the courage to dust off that old manuscript and give it another try. So, I poured myself into re-writing my story. The original version had been edited, but because I practically rewrote the book, I struggled with going back through the editing phase again. I took this to the Lord, and the most amazing thing happened. He encouraged me not to have it re-edited... to let it stand, and He would do the rest. He would ensure that people were blessed by the content, the message, and not be turned off by the grammar mistakes they were sure to find. I will be honest; it took me a while to be comfortable with this because I know it is stressed that the biggest turn-off when people read anything is when they find grammatical mistakes. Yet, I wanted to be authentic, real. I wanted others with the same disorder to put away their shame of the disorder and abandon themselves in the will and gift of God in their life. So, in June of 2019, my first book (The Other Side of Dyslexia) was published, mistakes and all. And I have never regretted that decision.

I also started a text ministry where I send out an encouraging word from the Lord to a group of people. I've discovered that the Lord has given me endless possibilities to write for Him. I plan to publish my third devotional in 2022 and just to keep things interesting, I'm working on courses to put online.

It's Never Over

As stated earlier, the possibilities are endless. It only takes an open, accessible heart to the Lord.

Side note: I started using Grammarly last year. I'm comfortable with this level of editing and believe that it doesn't take away from my need to express myself as a dyslexic writer.

So, you see, I am a Gospel Writer today because love must find a way to express itself. I love the Lord and I love writing to and for Him. I found that He always has someone for me to send words of encouragement, comfort, guidance, yes, even corrections to. But most of all, I became a Gospel Writer because it has given me a glimpse into the heart of God, and I get to share those intimate moments with you.

~Hope

THE GRACE TO BE AUTHENTIC

I MADE A PRAYERFUL DECISION NOT TO ALLOW ANY significant editing to take place in this book. You may wonder why… Well, I have dyslexia; therefore, I am a dyslexic writer. As with my website, I wanted this book to be a vehicle, a safe place that allows me to be me, Dyslexic.

So, if you come across a misspelled word, incorrect word, incorrect sentence structure, a comma out of place, and a host of other mistakes you're sure to find, celebrate with me. Why? Because God has taken away my shame, fear of failure, and, most of all, my fear of making mistakes when I write.

My prayer is that you will be blessed by God's grace as you read this book. I also pray that we will experience the power of Christ resting on us, for when we are weak, then He is strong. 2 Corinthians 12:8-10

INTRODUCTION

I firmly believe that the Lord is challenging us to rethink our position on faith and trust. Why? Because many people believe that God's sole mission is to prove to the world that He can be trusted.

In the bible, we find the following: *"And the LORD God commanded the man, saying, Of every tree of the garden thou mayest freely eat: But of the tree of the knowledge of good and evil, thou shalt not eat of it: for in the day that thou eatest thereof thou shalt surely die."* Genesis 2:16–17

At the tree of the knowledge of good and evil, Satan convinced Eve of the following:

- God is a withholder of good.
- God cannot be trusted.
- God is not fair.

And when the woman saw that the tree was good for food, and that it was pleasant to the eyes, and a tree to be desired to make one wise, she took of the fruit thereof, and did eat, and gave also unto her husband with her; and he did eat. Genesis 3:6

What did Adam and Eve gain by believing Satan's lies? They gain an experimental knowledge of evil, fear, and separation from God.

"And ye shall know the truth, and the truth shall make you free." John 8:32

Imagine what would happen each morning if we approached Christ firmly convinced of His faithfulness and trustworthiness. What would happen if we came to Christ with unwavering loyalty, faith, and confidence? We would daily experience the power and grace of God without measure as He intended.

Imagine what would happen if we believe that it is our privilege, our high calling, through the power of the Holy Spirit, to demonstrate our faithfulness to God.

Never doubt, the lies Satan convinced Adam and Eve are so engraved in our psyche that only the power of the Holy Spirit can dislodge them. And He will only do so with our permission. Those lies have shaped and significantly influenced our relationship with Christ. And once we acknowledge and accept that God is not a withholder of good, He is trustworthy, and He is fair, our lives will change.

That day in the garden, Adam and Eve wanted for nothing. Nothing. Yet Satan was able to convince them that God was withholding something vital, something good from them and they wanted it.

Now in God's great wisdom, He gave Adam and Eve the power of choice. The power to choose was entrusted to them, and they freely used it. However, this gift of choice was used unwisely, resulting in their removal from the garden and a world thrown into utter chaos. So who can't be trusted? Was it Adam and Eve or God?

In addition, the Lord proved His fairness and faithfulness by coming to this world, living among us, teaching and healing... He proved His love and faithfulness by dying on the cross, a death meant for you and me and now as our High Priest, He lives to make intercession on our behalf.

I think that's fair, don't you?

So how can we start turning things around? By remembering when we accepted Christ as our Saviour, we made a pledge to the Father, Son, and Holy Spirit to daily arm ourselves with the truth found in His word.

We agreed with Christ when He said:

I am that bread of life. John 6:48

He that believeth on Me, as the scripture hath said, out of his belly shall flow rivers of living water.
John 7:38

For what saith the scripture? Abraham believed God, and it was counted unto him for righteousness.
Romans 4:3

For the scripture saith, Whosoever believeth on Him shall not be ashamed. Romans 10:11

Wow! And in return for believing in Him, we have been entrusted with the gospel message and commission to tell the world of God's love, grace, and soon return.

> For God so loved the world, that He gave His only begotten Son, that whosoever believeth in Him should not perish, but have everlasting life. John 3:16–17

> For I am not ashamed of the gospel of Christ: for it is the power of God unto salvation to every one that believeth; to the Jew first, and also to the Greek. Romans 1:16

Furthermore, we have been entrusted with His name and His reputation.

Can Christ trust us to carry the gospel to those who do not know Him? Can Christ trust us to take care of His word, honor His name and bring glory to His mission? Can Christ trust us to face each day, adhering to His word and abiding in Him? Can He?

These are questions I encourage each of us to prayerfully answer. Why? Because if we question Christ's faithfulness as we face each day, as we exercise our right to choose, we may view our relationship with Christ through the lens of the deceptions presented to Adam and Eve.

The truth is, the Lord has given us the Holy Spirit to empower us to be faithful to Him by honoring Jesus's sacrifice... He has given us the Holy Spirit to help us bear fruit for Him and to live Christ's victorious life by sharing the gospel. I believe that's fair…

I pray that we courageously rethink our position on trust and our faithfulness to Christ.

As a writer, I enjoy sharing information that I hope and pray will challenge, encourage, support, and bring peace into someone's life. I know many people struggle with their faith, as I have. Yet, I hope we take a moment to reevaluate our position on who Christ is and how much we owe Him.

The following pages contain short daily devotionals designed to help us pause for a moment and think about how we can daily demonstrate our faithfulness to the One who loves us so much and gave up so much to be with us. Each page will challenge us to shift our gaze to the One who holds our hand and cares so much. His name is Jesus Christ, our Faithful Lord, Saviour, and Friend.

1

OUR NEED OF GOD

Imagine what will happen today if we acknowledge *our need of God* to show ourselves faithful in our time of need.

"BUT I AM POOR AND NEEDY; YET THE LORD THINKETH UPON me: Thou art my help and my deliverer; make no tarrying, O my God."

Are you feeling needy? What do you need from God as you face another day, another week? Do you need words of comfort, assurance? A hug? Do you need to know that God hasn't forgotten? Do you need to know that Christ's sacrifice is still available to you? Do you need to know that the gospel is real and that it is still the power of God unto salvation? Do you need to know that His thoughts towards you are still good? Do you need to know that you're not alone?

Trials uncover our deep need for God. And left covered, we may never bring our needs to God. Over time, our fears, self-sufficiency, and our need to be in control quiets the longing of the heart.

Then a trial comes, and things fall apart to remind us of our great need for God that was there all along.

"Is there no balm in Gilead; is there no physician there? why then is not the health of the daughter of my people recovered."

Good question. Why do we wait until a crisis blindsides us before we admit to God how much we need Him? Maybe a better question is, when will God be able to count on us to turn to Him in faith, petitioning Him for His abundant grace to remain faithful to Him during trials.

We keep demanding that God show Himself faithful before we believe. Ask yourself this question, when was the last time God failed to keep His word?

Remember, Jesus is the great Physician who does not practice medicine; He heals. He is the balm for the wounded, troubled heart. He will heal, restore, and redeem. But will we do our part by asking to be empowered by the Holy Spirit to remain faithful to Him… Will we show ourselves faithful by continually acknowledging and testifying to the world, those in our home, job, the marketplace of the love, grace, and mercy of Christ? The choice is ours…

Psalm 40:17; Romans 1:16,17; Jeremiah 29:11; Jeremiah 8:22; Luke 18:13-14

Dear Heavenly Father, may we always be found faithful to Thee. In Jesus's Name, Amen!

2

EVERLASTING ARM OF JESUS

> Imagine what will happen today if we lean on the strong, *everlasting arm of Jesus* to remain faithful to Him.

JESUS HAS PROMISED TO CARRY US AND GENTLY LEADS us. *"Ah Lord GOD! behold, Thou hast made the heaven and the earth by Thy great power and stretched out arm, and there is nothing too hard for Thee."*

The Word of God is a revealer of Christ's character. It is true; He is strong and mighty. He is our Creator, our Redeemer. So, when we are faced with a difficult situation, go to Jesus and lean on His strong arm, ask for the help needed to meet the day's need, and the faithfulness to wait for the deliverance of His promise.

Never should we be afraid to tell Jesus that we need Him and that we are glad He is in our *'everlasting Father'* (Isaiah 9:6).

It's okay to remind Him that He is your *Prince of Peace*, your great reward. Let Him know He makes your heart glad and that He is the lifter of your head.

Then remind yourself of the last time you told someone about the strong arm of Jesus? *"The LORD hath made bare His holy arm in the eyes of all the nations, and all the ends of the earth shall see the salvation of our God."* The gospel is not hidden; Jesus declared it from the cross. Now it is our turn to show ourselves faithful by telling someone that Jesus's arm is stretched out, ready to heal and save.

So, go ahead, lean on His strong arm, declare His salvation, that He is mighty to save. And tell them, when they face difficult situations, how Jesus strong arm made you strong, and you went out with His power to face the day. Tell them Christ did not turn you away empty. Tell them how He supplied your deepest needs. Tell them you have set your love upon Christ; therefore, He delivered you.

Isaiah 40:11; Jeremiah 32:17; Psalms 24:8; Genesis 1-3; Isaiah 52:10; Psalm 91:14

Dear Heavenly Father, may we always be found faithful to Thee. In Jesus's Name, Amen!

FAITHFUL

He giveth power to the faint; and to them that have no might he increaseth strength. Even the youths shall faint and be weary, and the young men shall utterly fall: But they that wait upon the LORD shall renew their strength; they shall mount up with wings as eagles; they shall run, and not be weary; and they shall walk, and not faint. Isaiah 40:29-31

3

COURAGE

Imagine what will happen today if we take *courage* from God to show ourselves faithful to Him no matter the trial.

KING DAVID SAID WHEN HE WAS FACING A DIFFICULT situation, *"I had fainted unless I had believed to see the goodness of the Lord in the land of the living. Wait on the Lord: be of good courage, and He shall strengthen thine heart: wait, I say, on the Lord."*

As you bow before the Lord, ask Him to give you the courage to wait on Him; to strengthen your heart while you wait... And the most amazing thing will happen, He will teach you how to worship Him while you wait. He will give you His courage to remain faithful to Him while you wait.

Isn't that amazing and exciting...

For Christ has promised, you won't wait alone nor in vain because He is worth the wait.

Psalm 27:13,14

4

GOD IS IN CONTROL

> Imagine what will happen today if we believe that *God is in control*.

"...TO THE INTENT THAT THE LIVING MAY KNOW THAT THE MOST High ruleth in the kingdom of men..." Daniel 4:17. Our hearts can find comfort in knowing God was in control yesterday. He is in control today. And He will be in control tomorrow. So, we can relax, rest, and show ourselves faithful when we face today, knowing that our sovereign Lord still reigns.

Armed with the truth, you can put away any complaints you may have aside; instead, share your heart with God. Just talk to Him as you would a trusted friend. The difference is His shoulders are big enough to carry, to hold whatever you share with Him.

Go ahead, tell Him what you are afraid of, what keeps you awake at night, and how scary the future seems. Tell Him why you struggle with being faithful to Him in times of trouble.

Yes, Jesus also wants to hear you tell Him what brought a smile to your face yesterday or this morning. He waits for you to tell Him how much you appreciate that He kept you safe last night while you slept and the beautiful sunrise or sunset you experienced.

The more we become comfortable talking to Him about everything, the more we will commit to Jesus. The more we will, with a humble, grateful heart demonstrate our faithfulness to Him, and find comfort knowing that He is in control.

Psalm 28:7; Psalm 34:2-4

Dear Heavenly Father, may we always be found faithful to Thee. In Jesus's Name, Amen!

FAITHFUL

Yet the LORD will command His lovingkindness in the daytime, and in the night His song shall be with me, and my prayer unto the God of my life.
Psalm 42:8

5

A HEART OF GRATITUDE

> Imagine what will happen today if we face today with *a heart of gratitude*, for God has been faithful in all His ways.

JESUS ALONE HAS KEPT US CLOTHED, FEED, AND SHELTERED. He is the great Shepherd, the great I AM. He is a very present help in time of need, and He inhabits our praise.

Where can you go that He is not already there? What hill will you climb that He has not already climbed? Whatever valley you will travel through, He has gone ahead and has cleared your path. He has already made provisions for everything that will affect you today. He has made it possible for us to show ourselves faithful to Him. Oh, what a Mighty God we serve.

So, as we go about our day, please note things we may have taken for granted. A warm coat to wear, a car that started this morning, a blue sky or rain. What about a door to lock, a plate to eat on, someone to love, a lamp to turn on, a couch to sit on, a window to look out through?

Oh, how blessed we are. When we are faithful to God, we will let our heart sing God's praise today in our smile, the task we're working on, in our conversations, how we dress, what we eat...

When we are faithful, we will give Him glory today by letting Him be known today in everything you do.

1 Corinthians 10:31; Psalm 138, 139

Dear Heavenly Father, may we always be found faithful to Thee. In Jesus's Name, Amen!

It takes courage to decide to be faithful to God, especially in difficult situations. However, it's important to remember that God equips and empowers us to be faithful to Him and remain loyal.

FAITHFUL

Hear my prayer, O LORD, give ear to my supplications: in Thy faithfulness answer me, and in Thy righteousness.
Psalm 143:1

6

THE STRENGTH OF THE ALMIGHTY

Imagine what will happen when we face today decidedly, intentionally relying in and on *the strength of the Almighty*.

JESUS HAS PROMISED TO GIVE US HIS STRENGTH SO THAT WE will run and not be weary, walk, and not faint. We can take refuge in the center of God's will, His grace, and His strength.

Today, let Jesus be your hiding place, your comfort zone, your strong tower. And as you kneel before God Almighty, find strength in knowing you are loved with an everlasting love. You are precious in His sight, and that His thoughts toward you are good and not evil.

It may surprise many that when we go to the Lord in faith, we show Him our faithfulness by taking hold of His strength. We show our commitment when we hold nothing back from Him. Nothing! We demonstrate our loyalty when we seek Him with all our hearts, mind, and soul.

Then see yourself sitting beside Him, lay your head on His shoulder, sigh relief, and rest. You are safe. You are comforted. You are taken care of. You are loved. You are strengthened, and He is worshipped. John 3:16.

> *Then he said unto them, Go your way, eat the fat, and drink the sweet, and send portions unto them for whom nothing is prepared: for this day is holy unto our Lord: neither be ye sorry; for the joy of the LORD is your strength.*
> *Nehemiah 8:10*

7

A FRIEND IN JESUS

Imagine what will happen today if we face today knowing that we have *a friend in Jesus*.

"HENCEFORTH I CALL YOU NOT SERVANTS; FOR THE SERVANT knoweth not what his lord doeth: but I have called you friends; for all things that I have heard of my Father I have made known unto you." Jesus was seeking to prepare His disciples to carry on His mission without His physical presence. He wanted them to know that they had a Friend in high places. And although He would not be with them bodily, His Spirit would never leave them.

Jesus is called by many names, *"...and His name shall be called Wonderful, Counsellor, The mighty God, The everlasting Father, The Prince of Peace."* Now He adds to this list, Friend.

Jesus is a Friend that has promised to walk with us in the valleys and help us climb mountain tops. He is a Friend that holds every secret we have and will never betray us.

A Friend that waits each morning to hear the sound of our voice. He is a very attentive Friend and knows the longing of our hearts even before we speak them. Oh, What a Friend we have in Jesus...

As a Friend, Jesus calls us to walk with Him, to show ourselves faithful by taking Him by the hand. Why? Because He has already gone where He will lead. He has lovingly measured out our day. He bids us trust, be faithful, and rest in His friendship, for He longs to give us purpose and to enrich our lives today so that others will desire His friendship as well. Oh, What a Friend we have in Jesus...

John 15:15; Isaiah 9:6; Psalm 139

Dear Heavenly Father, may we always be found faithful to Thee. In Jesus's Name, Amen!

FAITHFUL

Be careful for nothing; but in every thing by prayer and supplication with thanksgiving let your requests be made known unto God.
Philippians 4:6

8

OUR REDEEMER LIVES

Imagine what will happen if we face today knowing that *our Redeemer lives*.

"O Lord, Thou hast pleaded the causes of my soul; Thou hast redeemed my life." To redeem is to purchase back; to ransom, to liberate. Jesus demonstrated His love for us by redeeming our life, by willingly giving up His. He has no regrets. Lamentations 3:58

Do you question your worth? If so, remember the life He lived, then stand next to the cross and stay there until His sacrifice becomes real to you. Then visit the tomb where they laid His bruised, torn body. Wait there until you see with the eye of faith the angels rolling the stone away and hear the Father calling His name. Watch Him come forth out of the tomb, gloried. Then cast yourself down at His feet and worship the King.

Jesus rescues still. He delivers still. He liberates still. He is Mighty still. Praise Christ for willingly paying our redemptive price. And He stands with all power to enable us to remain faithful to Him, the One who gave us life.

Psalm 71:23; 86: 12; 107:8.

> *I will praise Thee, O Lord my God, with all my heart: and I will glorify Thy name for evermore. For great is Thy mercy toward me: and Thou hast delivered my soul from the lowest hell.*
> *Psalm 86:12-13*

9

GOD MEETS ALL OUR NEEDS

Imagine what will happen today if we face today, knowing that *God can meet all our needs.*

JESUS IS OMNIPOTENT (ALMIGHTY, ALL-POWERFUL). No matter how relentless the enemy may be right now, God is near. For He promised, *"The LORD is nigh unto them that are of a broken heart; and saveth such as be of a contrite spirit. Many are the afflictions of the righteous: but the LORD delivereth him out of them all."*

David said the LORD will deliver us from "all" our afflictions, not some, but all. Who can make that promise and keep it? Only Jesus!

David also said, *"I waited patiently for the LORD, and He inclined unto me and heard my cry. He brought me up also out of a horrible pit, out of the miry clay, and set my feet upon a rock and established my goings. And He hath put a new song in my mouth, even praise unto our God: many shall see it, and fear, and shall trust in the LORD."* How did David demonstrate His faithfulness to God?

By giving testimony that he would wait and trust in the Lord until He brought him out of that pit and firmly set his feet upon a Rock.

David doesn't say how long he waited, but what we do know is that God gave David the strength and faith to remain faithful to Him. And at the right time, God delivered him out of a horrible pit as He promised He would. Hallelujah, Hallelujah our Lord reigns.

Psalm 34:18-19; 40:1-3; 1 Peter 5:6-7

Dear Heavenly Father, may we always be found faithful to Thee. In Jesus's Name, Amen!

FAITHFUL

Continue in prayer, and watch in the same with thanksgiving...
Colossians 4:2

10

MIGHTY CONFIDENCE

Imagine what will happen if we face today with *confidence* that Jesus will be our *mighty confidant*.

JESUS IS THE PERSON WITH WHOM YOU CAN SHARE YOUR JOYS, sorrows, cares, and fears. He will hold your secret; He will not betray you. His greatest joy is to intercede for you. To present you to the Father. *"I pray for them: I pray not for the world, but for them which Thou hast given me; for they are Thine. And all Mine are Thine, and Thine are Mine, and I am glorified in them. ... I have given them Thy word; and the world hath hated them, because they are not of the world, even as I am not of the world. I pray not that Thou shouldest take them out of the world, but that Thou shouldest keep them from the evil. ... Sanctify them through Thy truth: Thy word is truth. ... Neither pray I for these alone, but for them also which shall believe on Me through their word."*

Through Christ, we learn to pray with confidence for ourselves and others. In addition, through the power of the Holy Spirit, we are to demonstrate our loyalty toward God in moments of joys and sorrows. Why? *"For we have not an high priest which cannot be touched with the feeling of our infirmities; but was in all points tempted like as we are, yet without sin. Let us, therefore, come boldly unto the throne of grace, that we may obtain mercy, and find grace to help in time of need."*

When is there a time we don't need Jesus? Therefore, with boldness, humility, and confidence, approach God's throne of grace. Because He is, *"... the King eternal, immortal, invisible, the only wise God who bid you entrance to His presence."* And what will you find there? *"Thou wilt shew me the path of life: in Thy presence is fulness of joy; at Thy right hand there are pleasures for evermore."*

John 17:9-10, 14-15, 17, 20; Psalm 16:11; Hebrews 4:15-16; 1 Timothy 1:17

Dear Heavenly Father, may we always be found faithful to Thee. In Jesus's Name, Amen!

FAITHFUL

Blessed be God, even the Father of our Lord Jesus Christ, the Father of mercies, and the God of all comfort; Who comforteth us in all our tribulation, that we may be able to comfort them which are in any trouble, by the comfort wherewith we ourselves are comforted of God.
2 Corinthians 1:3-4

This trial that you're passing through is a wonderful opportunity to demonstrate your faithfulness, loyalty to God by making a decision to put your trust in Him no matter the difficulty of the trial or the outcome. Why? When we are faithful to God we demonstrate our trust in His power to meet our needs and take care of us during a trial.

11

JESUS'S VICTORIOUS LIFE

Imagine what will happen today if we claim *Jesus's victorious life*.

"*O SING UNTO THE LORD A NEW SONG; FOR HE HATH DONE marvellous things: His right hand, and His holy arm, hath gotten Him the victory.*" What do you need victory over? Whatever it is, He has already fought and won that battle. That is why He bids you come, "*boldly unto the throne of grace, that you may obtain mercy, and find grace to help in time of need.*" He has promised to be "*your refuge and strength, a very present help in trouble.*"

There is a catch. You will have to trust the battle to the Lord. No more taking it to Him, then taking it back. With the eye of faith, do you see Christ's right hand, His holy arm stretching out to you, ready to receive what troubles you? Why then walk away, leaving Jesus empty-handed? If you don't know how to let it go, tell Him. 'Father, I give You permission to take it because I don't know how to let it go.

Take my heart; keep my heart. It is Yours. I acknowledge that I belong to You. You created me and redeemed me.

You paid too great a price for me to continue refusing to accept Your right hand, Your strong holy arm, Your victorious life. Please take the thing that troubles my heart, and in exchange, please give me the victory I have longed for.'

When we do this, we demonstrate to God that He can trust us to turn to Him in prayer. Then we are open to His timing and methods, and we see the salvation of the Lord. He will instruct us in battle, and through the power of the Holy Spirit will are obedient.

In addition, He will tell us what part we are to play in the battle. He will give us His strength and courage to climb any mountain that He chooses not to move. Therefore, faithfully take hold of Christ's right hand, His holy, strong, loving, caring arm that He ever extends to us.

And when you grasp it, hold on as if your life depended on it because it does. So, go ahead, sing a new song, for He has done marvelous things, He has gotten the victory.

Don't keep Christ waiting; He longs to hear you sing.

Psalm 98:1; Hebrew 4:16; Psalm 46:1

Dear Heavenly Father, may we always be found faithful to Thee. In Jesus's Name, Amen!

12

GOD'S FAITHFULNESS

Imagine what will happen today if we *rest in God's faithfulness*.

JESUS'S COURAGE. HIS STRENGTH. HIS LOVE IS REASON enough for us to remain steadfast and committed to Him. The fact that He never slumbers nor sleeps. He is never caught off guard nor paces around heaven; wringing His hands, wondering what He shall do to help us through our situation, gives us the freedom and courage we need to prove ourselves unwavering in our trust towards Him.

Listen to these comforting words and be encouraged: *"Fear thou not; for I am with thee: be not dismayed; for I am thy God: I will strengthen thee; yea, I will help thee; yea, I will uphold thee with the right hand of My righteousness. ... For I, the LORD thy God will hold thy right hand, saying unto thee, Fear not; I will help thee."*

He doesn't want us to be afraid or dismayed. He is the great comforter, our strength, our help.

Therefore, take Him by the hand in faith, resting, trusting, believing that He will do what is best and good.

We serve a conquering King. He does not lose battles. His death on the cross was not a defeat but a victory. He proved that He is more powerful than Satan. His victory is ours; all we must do is believe.

Then chose to walk with Him. Share with Him that thing that troubles you the most. You cannot weary Him, for He has promised, *'I will strengthen thee; yea, I will help thee; yea, I will uphold thee with the right hand of My righteousness.'* You can trust whatever God says, for He has also promised, *"My covenant will I not break, nor alter the thing that is gone out of My lips."*

O magnify the Lord with me, and let us praise His name together.

Isaiah 41:10, 13; Psalm 89:34

Dear Heavenly Father, may we always be found faithful to Thee. In Jesus's Name, Amen!

FAITHFUL

Know therefore that the LORD thy God, He is God, the faithful God, which keepeth covenant and mercy with them that love Him and keep His commandments to a thousand generations...
Deuteronomy 7:9

13

GOD'S LOVE

Imagine what will happen today if we know that *God's loves* is measureless and everlasting.

"For God so loved the world, that He gave His only begotten Son, that whosoever believeth in Him should not perish, but have everlasting life."

As we meditate upon the love of God today and the love He has for us... And as we search the scriptures diligently to understand His mercy and grace... We realize that God's love for us is to wondrous for us to grasp.

Everything He had done, is doing, will do is an expression of His love for us. That is why Paul can say without hesitation, *"For I am persuaded, that neither death, nor life, nor angels, nor principalities, nor powers, nor things present, nor things to come, Nor height, nor depth, nor any other creature, shall be able to separate us from the love of God, which is in Christ Jesus our Lord."*

How does one respond to such love? We daily renew our allegiance to Christ through the power of the Holy Spirit. We honor and obey Him by faithfully serving Him and others.

We respond through faith, resting in the comfort of His love and strength, knowing that we are fearlessly loved by God, our Creator, Redeemer, and Friend.

John 3:16; Romans 8:38-39

> *Dear Heavenly Father, may we always be found faithful to Thee. In Jesus's Name, Amen!*

14

NOT FORSAKEN OF GOD

> Imagine what will happen if we face today with full assurance that we are *not forsaken of God*.

WE MAY BE TROUBLED ON EVERY SIDE, BUT WE ARE NOT distressed when we look to Jesus. We may be perplexed about life, but we are not in despair when we look to Jesus. We may be persecuted, but when we look to Jesus, we know we are not forsaken. We may be cast down, but when we look to Jesus, we know He won't allow us to be destroyed.

Hard times are our opportunity to be empowered by the Holy Spirit to persevere in a trial. Why? Because as a Christian, we always carry the marks of Jesus's death in our bodies so that His victorious life is manifest in ours.

"I am crucified with Christ: nevertheless I live; yet not I, but Christ liveth in me: and the life which I now live in the flesh I live by the faith of the Son of God, who loved me, and gave Himself for me." This blessed assurance can be yours today.

2 Corinthians 4:8-10; Galatians 2:20

FAITHFUL

We are troubled on every side, yet not distressed; we are perplexed, but not in despair; Persecuted, but not forsaken; cast down, but not destroyed; Always bearing about in the body the dying of the Lord Jesus, that the life also of Jesus might be made manifest in our body.
2 Corinthians 4:8-10

15

FEARLESS

Imagine what will happen if we face today *fearless* in Christ.

"For I the LORD thy God will hold thy right hand, saying unto thee, Fear not; I will help thee." What can happen today that God has not already faced and conquered? *"The LORD shall go forth as a mighty man, He shall stir up jealousy like a man of war: He shall cry, yea, roar; He shall prevail against His enemies."* Why? *"For God hath not given us the spirit of fear; but of power, and of love, and of a sound mind."*

Consider making a commitment to Christ today that you will take hold of His hand. Walk with Him. Talk to Him. Trust Him. Believe Him. When you do, His peace will cover you today while He fights and win every battle you will face today, and you will hear Him say, *'I am your God. I will hold your right hand...fear not; I will help thee.'* O magnify the LORD with me, and let us exalt His name together.

Isaiah 41:13; Isaiah 42:13; 2 Timothy 1:7; Psalm 34:3

The Friendship Jesus offers us is life-transforming. He wants to be our forever Friend. So, when our earthy friends despise and forsake us, we will faithfully take it to our Friend in prayer. In His arms, He'll take and shield us… We will always find a solace there. Oh, What A Friend we have in Jesus…

FAITHFUL

Yea, though I walk through the valley of the shadow of death, I will fear no evil: for Thou art with me; Thy rod and Thy staff they comfort me. Psalm 23:4

16

QUIETNESS AND CONFIDENT

Imagine what will happen today if we in quietness and confidence claim Christ as our hope and anchor.

CHRIST HAS PROMISED TO PREACH THE GOSPEL TO THE POOR, to heal the brokenhearted, to preach deliverance to those who are being held captive by sin and circumstances, to recover sight to those who are spiritually blind, to set at liberty them that are bruised by life experiences, to open prison doors of the heart. He has promised to comfort all those who mourn in trial and sorrow.

Christ is looking for those who are ready to faithfully and confidently make an exchange. For this to take place, we must meet Him at the cross. He longs to give us beauty for ashes, the oil of joy for mourning, and the garment of praise for the spirit of heaviness. He will do this so that we might be called trees of righteousness, the planting of the LORD, that He might be glorified.

Heavenly Father, as I kneel before Your throne of grace, I stretch out my hands to You, for You stretched out Yours on the cross for me. Lord, I'll be honest, I'm struggling to surrender my heart to You, yet I know I must. I know not how. I, therefore, consent for You to take it, keep it pure, it is Yours. May every step I take today to be a step taken with You. I consent to take Your strength and courage, to cling to the cross, yet live in the power of Your resurrection. I'm so thankful that Your greatest joy is to intercede on my behalf. Thank You for creating in me a clean heart and putting in me Your spirit. In Jesus Precious Name. Amen!

Isaiah 61; Luke 4; Isaiah 61:3; Ezekiel 36

17

CHRIST'S VICTORIOUS LIFE

> Imagine what will happen today if by faith we claim as our own *Christ's victorious life*.

WHAT MUST I DO TO RECEIVE HIS LIFE? DAILY, UNWAVERING surrender. It requires us to faithfully come, boldly, yet humbly before God's throne, confessing our great need for Christ and our dependency on Him. It requires a distrust of self and total reliance upon Him. Let there be found in our walk with Christ today, constantly watching unto prayer, a drawing closer and closer to the Savior's side.

So, what will this do for us? We will be in possession of the power of the gospel. The apostle Paul said that he was not ashamed of the gospel of Christ. Why? *"...for it is the power of God unto salvation to everyone that believes... For therein is the righteousness of God revealed from faith to faith: as it is written, the just shall live by faith."*

What is the gospel? It is the life, death, burial, and resurrection of Christ. Why is it so powerful? When we shift our gaze from the world, we see the uplifted cross, and we are drawn by the power of Christ to accept His victorious life. We acknowledge that we cannot save ourselves; we could not pay our debt; Christ has done this for us.

By unwavering faith in Christ, His victorious life now becomes ours…His strength and courage now become ours. His faithfulness now becomes ours. His obedience to the commandments of God now becomes ours.

How can this be? *"For you are dead, and your life is hidden with Christ in God," "...and the life which you now live in the flesh you live by the faith of the Son of God, who loved you, and gave Himself for you."* Self is crucified daily by renouncing the love of the world. You now have room in your life for Christ's victorious life.

We have made peace with God through the blood of the cross, and we are reconciled to God. We are one with Christ. All that is required is that we continue in our faith, become grounded and settled, and be not moved away from the hope of the gospel, which we have heard, and which was preached to us.

The power of Christ's resurrected life is ours by faith. We are now in possession of the power of the gospel to live Christ's victorious life.

Now isn't that good news!

Romans 1:16-17; 1 Corinthians 15; Colossians 3:3; Galatian 2:20; Colossians 3; Colossians 1:23

Dear Heavenly Father, may we always be found faithful to Thee. In Jesus's Name, Amen!

FAITHFUL

I will praise Thee, O LORD, with my whole heart; I will shew forth all Thy marvellous works.

Psalm 9:1

18

ALL CONTROLS

> Imagine what will happen today if we place *all controls* in the mighty hand of God.

TAKE COURAGE WHEN LIFE SEEMS OUT OF CONTROL, remembering and acknowledging that God is sovereign. He bids us to boldly yet humbly come into His presence, to come before His throne of grace to receive mercy, to acknowledge our need of Him.

So, with confidence, unwavering Holy Spirit grace, take your eyes off your current situation (your wayward child, that bill that needs to be paid, that unwanted diagnosis, that unfaithful spouse, that layoff from your job, etc.) and remember who God is and who you have given all your controls over to.

God is Omnipotent; there is no limit to His power. He is Omnipresent; there is no place He is not. He is the great I AM. He is Omniscient, and there is nothing He doesn't already know (your past, present, and future) about you.

So, what is holding you back from giving Him your whole heart, withholding nothing from Him? Think about it...Who knew the choices you would make and still said, *"Let there be light."* Who knows everything about you and still sent His Son to die in your place? Who? Who knows all about that place inside your heart that holds secrets, dark secrets, yet He continues to draw you to Himself with His lovingkindness? Who alone knows your deepest needs, greatest sorrow, highest joy?

Who? Who waits patiently for you to bow the knee in total submission to His will and His word? Who has not given up on you and is not ashamed to acknowledge you as His own? Who?

His name is Jesus, Wonderful, Counselor, the mighty God, the everlasting Father, the Prince of Peace.

Face today with confidence, knowing that God is in control. Hallelujah!

Hebrews 10:35-37; Genesis 1:1

Dear Heavenly Father, may we always be found faithful to Thee. In Jesus's Name, Amen!

19

WHEN WE ARE AFRAID

> Imagine what will happen today if we take Christ's courage and believe, *"What time I am afraid, I will trust in Thee."*

THAT FOUR-LETTER WORD, FEAR, CAN IMMOBILIZE A person. It can cause our thinking to short circuit. And if fear is our constant companion, it will interfere with our trust and our faithfulness to God.

When fear hang over our head like a cloud, eating away at our hearts and souls, we have replaced God's perfect love with fear, and it becomes our blind spot and the lens we see the world.

What can we do? We can tell Jesus what we're afraid of, even if we must do it a hundred times, don't let go until God is in full possession of our fears. Then He will give us the courage to tell fear:

"The LORD is my light and my salvation; whom shall I fear? the LORD is the strength of my life; of whom shall I be afraid... For God hath not given us the spirit of fear; but of power, and of love, and of a sound mind." Why? Because "There is no fear in love; but perfect love casteth out fear: because fear hath torment. He that feareth is not made perfect in love."

Let God's perfect love take custody of your heart, and watch God's perfect love cast, throw, fling fear out of your heart. He can do it. He will do it. *"Therefore fear thou not, O my servant Jacob, saith the LORD; neither be dismayed, O Israel: for, lo, I will save thee from afar, and thy seed from the land of their captivity; and Jacob shall return, and shall be in rest, and be quiet, and none shall make him afraid."*

Psalm 56:3; Psalm 27:1; 2 Timothy 1:7; 1 John 4:18; Jeremiah 30:10

Dear Heavenly Father, may we always be found faithful to Thee. In Jesus's Name, Amen!

FAITHFUL

The LORD is my strength and my shield; my heart trusted in Him, and I am helped: therefore my heart greatly rejoiceth; and with my song will I praise Him.
Psalm 28:7

20

TOTAL RELIANCE

Imagine what will happen today if we *completely rely* on the One who speaks, and the sun rises and sets, flowers open and close, oceans hold fast, and birds sing His praises.

KING DAVID REMINDS US THAT THE HEAVENS DECLARE HIS glory and because the Lord reigns, we should rejoice and be glad.

But suppose you find yourself anxious and afraid, lonely and troubled, disillusioned and doubtful, facing what appears to be insurmountable odds, a mountain that seems too difficult to climb. In that case, Christ encourages us through His Spirit to remain faithful and claim His promises: *"And the LORD shall guide thee continually, and satisfy thy soul in drought, and make fat thy bones: and thou shalt be like a watered garden, and like a spring of water, whose waters fail not."*

Christ has demonstrated His love and mercy toward us; now, it's our turn to do the same for Him. And when we do, we will know better the peace of our heavenly Father, the maker of heaven and earth. We will tell others of Jesus our Redeemer, protector, provider, healer, sustainer, Saviour, Lord, and Friend. Isaiah 58:11

> And this is the confidence that we have in Him, that, if we ask any thing according to His will, He heareth us: And if we know that He hear us, whatsoever we ask, we know that we have the petitions that we desired of Him.
> 1 John 5:14-15

When a trial, temptation or hardship presents itself, offer it up to God as a freewill offering. A sacrifice that He will use to fit us for a greater work. When doing so, we show our faithfulness to the One who offered Himself, the greatest sacrifice.

FAITHFUL

*For I reckon that the
sufferings of this present time
are not worthy to be
compared with the glory
which shall be revealed in us.
Romans 8:18*

21

PRINCE OF PEACE

> Imagine what will happen today if we believe that Jesus is the *Prince of Peace*.

WHAT IS PEACE? TO BE COMPLETE, SECURE IN WHO CHRIST IS and what He has done. The prophet Isaiah described Christ as *"The Prince of Peace."* He also said of Christ, *"Thou wilt keep him in perfect peace, whose mind is stayed on Thee: because he trusteth in Thee."* Jesus said, *Peace I leave with you, My peace I give unto you: not as the world giveth, give I unto you. Let not your heart be troubled, neither let it be afraid."* Isaiah 26:3; Isaiah 9:6; Christ bids us take hold of His completeness, His perfect peace because it's transforming. In response, we seek Him to demonstrate our loyalty to Him for all that He has done. *"Be careful for nothing; but in everything by prayer and supplication with thanksgiving let your requests be made known unto God. And the peace of God, which passeth all understanding, shall keep your hearts and minds through Christ Jesus."* John 14:27; Philippians 4:6-7

22

PEACE OF GOD

> Imagine what will happen today when we let the *Peace of God* rule our heart.

WHEN JESUS LEFT THIS WORLD AND RETURNED TO HIS heavenly kingdom, He left the gift of peace with us. *"Peace I leave with you, My peace I give unto you: not as the world giveth, give I unto you. Let not your heart be troubled, neither let it be afraid."* What have you done with His gift? Does His gift, wrapped in a beautiful box, sit on the shelf of your heart unopened? Do you take it down from time to time, admire how beautiful the wrappings are, but fear to open it? Have you given any consideration to the cost of His gift?

The word of God reveals to us that Christ counted the cost of His gift, walked out of heaven, and submitted to a life of poverty, hardship, and ridicule. If that wasn't enough, Christ took a beating; He never said a word, paid the price so that you and I would know His peace for *"...the chastisement of our peace was upon Him."*

So please stop! Pause for a moment. Put aside what is troubling you this morning and think about how much Christ wants you to know His peace, that He gladly died to be able to hand you this gift. Oh, what love! Oh, what love!

Out of all the gifts you will receive today, this month, this year, don't let another day go by and leave God's gift of His Son's peace unopened. It is a gift that is meant to be opened and worn every season. It will never go out of style. It is a gift that fits you perfectly and always will.

It is a gift meant to be displayed for others to see, desire, and desire. This gift is your life's fragrance. It is a gift that defies logic to those who know your circumstances. Oh, what loves the Father has for us.

Out of all the gifts you can give to someone, today will be the story of the Peace giver, how His sacrifice is the reason you have peace.

Face today, knowing that the peace of God is yours. So, go ahead and open the box, and hear the Father say, *"How beautiful upon the mountains are the feet of him that bringeth good tidings, that publisheth peace; that bringeth good tidings of good, that publisheth salvation; that saith unto Zion, Thy God reigneth!"*

John 14:27; Isaiah 53:4; Isaiah 52:7

Dear Heavenly Father, may we always be found faithful to Thee. In Jesus's Name, Amen!

FAITHFUL

*And my tongue shall speak of
Thy righteousness and of Thy
praise all the day long.
Psalm 35:28*

23

FEARLESSLY LOVED

Imagine what will happen today if we believe we are *fearlessly loved* by Christ our Saviour.

LET THE TRUTH OF GOD'S LOVE FOR YOU WRAP AROUND YOU like a soft, warm garment. Settle into it... Rest. For He cares for you.

The Spirit of God is bidding us come with our whole heart to Jesus today, for He has promised, *Come unto Me all ye who are weary and heavy of heart...take My yoke and learn of Me... I will give you rest.* How? By taking Christ by the hand, walking where He leads, which will always be on a path that leads to His throne of grace. Matthew 28:30

Grace is God's power to overcome sin and any obstacle we may face. So be consciously, intentionally aware that the God we kneel before today spoke and it was done (created all things), breathed life into a lifeless form (Adam), spoke to a raging sea and it was stilled, drove demons out of a man's son, and refused to come down off the cross because we were on His mind.

Jesus lives, and because He lives, there is nothing that will happen today that we will not be able to face with His courage. Let the Spirit of courage, faithfulness, and peace rule our hearts today.

Isaiah 49:15; 1 John 1:7; John 3:16,17

Dear Heavenly Father, may we always be found faithful to Thee. In Jesus's Name, Amen!

> Can a woman forget her sucking child, that she should not have compassion on the son of her womb? yea, they may forget, yet will I not forget thee. Behold, I have graven thee upon the palms of My hands; thy walls are continually before Me.
> Isaiah 49:15-16

24

GLORIFIED REDEEMER

Imagine what will happen today if we keep our eyes fixed on our *glorified Redeemer*.

HALLELUJAH! CHRIST HAS ALREADY WON EVERY BATTLE WE will face today. Remember when the children of Israel left Egypt and reached an impasse. They stood before the Red Sea, mountains on each side, and Pharaoh's army racing towards them. They had no choice but to stand still; there was no other place to go.

When God tells us to be still (Psalm 46), are we determined to faithfully obey Him? Some of us don't like standing still. We feel out of control, and this often leads to complaining like the children of Israel, *"And in the morning, then ye shall see the glory of the LORD; for that He heareth your murmurings against the LORD: and what are we, that ye murmur against us?"* Exodus 16:7

How quickly we forget who has led us, yes, even through wilderness places. Who allows us to stand before a raging sea with mountains on both sides and the enemy (Dementia, Alzheimer, poor health, wayward children, past due bills, failed marriages) racing towards us?

What was Moses's response? *"The LORD shall fight for you, and ye shall hold your peace."* He also told them, don't be afraid, stand still, this enemy you shall see no more. What was the Lord's response? Move forward into the sea; you shall walk on dry ground through the midst of the sea.

God pleads with us to fix our eyes on Christ, our glorified Redeemer. Walk by faith where God leads. Trust His timing to part the Red Sea. Place in His nail-pierced hands that which troubles your soul. When you do, you will sing the song of Moses, *"I will sing unto the LORD, for He hath triumphed gloriously...The LORD is my strength and song, and He is become my salvation: He is my God... and I will exalt Him. The LORD is a man of war: the LORD is His name... Who is like unto thee, O LORD, among the gods?"*

Exodus 13-14; Exodus 14:11-12; Exodus 14:13, 14; Exodus 15,16

Dear Heavenly Father, may we always be found faithful to Thee. In Jesus's Name, Amen!

FAITHFUL

Why art Thou cast down, O my soul? and why art Thou disquieted in me? hope Thou in God: for I shall yet praise Him for the help of His countenance.
Psalm 42:5

25

STRENGTH OF THE LORD

Imagine what will happen if we face today in the *strength of the Lord*,

---

"I WILL GO IN THE STRENGTH OF THE LORD GOD: I WILL MAKE mention of Thy righteousness, even of Thine only." How did David go in the strength of the Lord? By praising God for His mighty acts. His goodness. His righteousness. His love and power to save.

When we stop to remember who we serve, who we make our petitions to, who is watching over us, who alone can save us, deliver us, restore us, and redeem us… We lift our hands and heart in praise, renewing our allegiance to the Holy One, and we know we are strengthened for the day.

Christ died on the cross made it possible to face today with our backs straight.

We take His courage and wear it like a cloak around us, and we remember, *"Thine, O LORD, is the greatness, and the power, and the glory, and the victory, and the majesty: for all that is in the heaven and in the earth is Thine; Thine is the kingdom, O LORD, and Thou art exalted as head above all...*

Both riches and honour come of Thee, and Thou reignest over all; and in Thine hand is power and might; and in Thine hand it is to make great, and to give strength unto all. Now therefore, our God, we thank Thee, and praise Thy glorious name." O magnify the Lord with me and let us exalt His name together.

Psalm 71:15-16; 1 Chronicles 29:11-13

Dear Heavenly Father, may we always be found faithful to Thee. In Jesus's Name, Amen!

Through submission, we put on display our loyalty, faithfulness to Christ. In exchange His precious promises are ours. Surrender and submit to the mighty love and power of God. He bids us take His yoke. He bids us learn of Him. He bids us take up His life of obedience. He bids us trust Him to walk with Him. He bids us let Him lighten our burdens.

FAITHFUL

Why art Thou cast down, O my soul? and why art Thou disquieted in me? hope Thou in God: for I shall yet praise Him for the help of His countenance.
Psalm 42:5

26

THE YOKE OF CHRIST

Imagine what will happen today if we *wear Christ's yoke*.

"TAKE MY YOKE UPON YOU, AND LEARN OF ME; FOR I AM MEEK and lowly in heart: and ye shall find rest unto your souls. For My yoke is easy, and My burden is light." Christ bids us, take His yoke, which will bring us close to His side. We will move in step with Him. We will be taught of Him and experience what it means to rest in Him.

The yoke also represents submission. Don't let that word 'submission' scare you. Just remember who is offering to carry the heaviest part of the burden. Remember who said His yoke is light? Who has said that if we take His yoke, we shall find rest? It's Jesus.

Aren't you tired of trying to bear your burdens alone? Aren't you tired of trying to figure it all out by yourself? Then go to God, fall at His feet and tell Him you're ready to exchange your yoke for His. Tell Him you don't know how to let it go; however, you permit Him to take it.

Tell Him how tired you are, that you have been trying to do something that you were never designed to carry or called to do.

Tell Him you're sorry for denying His outstretched hand, biding you to come so that He could help carry your load. Ask Him to abide in you that you may abide in Him. Then claim His victorious life, then spend the rest of your life working alongside Him to build up His kingdom.

Let today be the day that we daily faithfully take Christ's yoke and experience freedom, a lightness in our step, a peace in our hearts that we have longed for. Let us do it today!

Matthew 11:29-30

Dear Heavenly Father, may we always be found faithful to Thee. In Jesus's Name, Amen!

27

THE GOODNESS OF THE LORD

Imagine what will happen today if we remember the *goodness of our Lord Jesus Christ.*

WE ARE FAITHFUL TO GOD WHEN WE REMEMBER THE goodness of God.

So, let's take a moment to walk down memory lane. Remember when Jesus called the disciples to leave their secular occupation to follow Him? And they did. Their lives were never the same. Remember when He preached on a hillside the foundation and organization of His government. The title of His sermon that day was *"Blessed are Thou..."* Remember when He healed the leper, the Centurion's servant, and Peter's mother-in-law. When He rebuked the storm on the lake, delivered the two possessed demoniacs of Gadara, healed the paralytic man that was lowered from Peter's roof, answered questions about fasting, and restored health to Jairus' daughter. Remember when He met a woman at a well and gave her living water.

Do you remember when He taught, preached, and healed all manner of sickness and disease and His famed reaches far beyond the borders of Galilee? Remember when He prayed in the garden and drops of blood ran down His face.

Remember that He went without food, sleep, that unkind words were spoken to Him? Remember how tired He was and that His body was severely lacerated. Remember that He offered His broken body to purchase our life. He died the death that we should have died so that we could live the life He came to give.

Do you remember that no one demonstrated tender mercies toward Him, and as He was stretched out on a cross and nails were cruelly driven into His hands and feet that He murmured not a word?

Remember that we forsook Him in His greatest hour and left Him alone to die in our place. Do you remember?

Has your desire to prove your faithfulness to Christ been restored? Then approach Jesus this morning to renew your allegiance to Him by telling Jesus how much you love Him. How much you appreciate His sacrifice and all the things He has done for you. Let Him know how much you appreciate His strength and courage and redemptive power. Thank Him for not staying in the grave, that you have taken courage in His resurrection power.

Jeremiah 17:7; Psalm 34:3

Dear Heavenly Father, may we always be found faithful to Thee. In Jesus's Name, Amen!

FAITHFUL

Be careful for nothing; but in every thing by prayer and supplication with thanksgiving let your requests be made known unto God. And the peace of God, which passeth all understanding, shall keep your hearts and minds through Christ Jesus.
Philippians 4:6–7

28

TRANSFORMING POWER OF GOD

Imagine what will happen today if we *acknowledge the power of God.*

A NOBLEMAN CAME TO JESUS TO REQUEST THAT HE HEAL HIS son. *Jesus responded by saying, "Except ye see signs and wonders, ye will not believe."* John 4:48. Jesus is more desirous to give us greater blessings than that which we have asked for. But we are not prepared to receive it.

What did Jesus know about this man? He came to Jesus, not with a heart of faith, but a heart that would believe on one condition, that He heal his, then he would believe that Jesus was who He said He was.

Don't you love it when Jesus shows us our true condition before Him? When He does, it is an opportunity, beautifully carve out by Jesus to humble ourselves before Him, confess our lack of faith, repent, and receive.

Unfortunately, when Jesus delays answering our prayer, we are prone to doubt, to give up. So, what is Jesus doing?

When we don't get what we have asked for, or the answer does not come when we wanted it to, our reaction reveals the hidden things of the heart and our deep need for Christ's transforming grace. He helps us denounce our unfaithfulness, selfishness and confess our great need for Him.

The nobleman had a decision to make. He had to take Christ at His word or lose the blessing he sought. So, he asked again, but his time, his request was grounded in faith, *"Sir, come down ere my child die. Jesus saith unto him, Go thy way; thy son liveth. And the man believed the word that Jesus had spoken unto him, and he went his way."* John 4:49-50, 53.

Don't be discouraged if the answer to your petition is delayed.

Thank God for doing a greater work in the heart so when the answer comes, our hearts are ready to receive more than we ask for.

> *Dear Heavenly Father, may we always be found faithful to Thee. In Jesus's Name, Amen!*

29

LIGHT OF CHRIST'S LOVE, MERCY, AND GRACE

Imagine what will happen today if we step into the *Light of Christ's love*, mercy, and grace.

WE ARE ENCOURAGED TO SET OUR AFFECTIONS UPON CHRIST, not just once, but daily and to seek Him with all our heart, mind, and soul. Trust in Him. Rely on Him. We are encouraged to talk faith and never doubt His loving care.

Sound simple. So why do we struggle? The answer is also simple; we question if Christ can be trusted.

"The LORD also will be a refuge for the oppressed, a refuge in times of trouble. And they that know Thy name will put their trust in Thee: for Thou, LORD, hast not forsaken them that seek Thee." Psalm 9: 9,10.

Moses demonstrated his faithfulness to the Lord by requesting God to show him His glory. Moses's prayed, *"... shew me now Thy way, that I may know Thee..."*

And the Lord's response was, *"I will make all My goodness pass before Thee, and I will proclaim the name of the LORD before thee; and will be gracious to whom I will be gracious, and will shew mercy on whom I will shew mercy."* Exodus 33:13, 19.

Was Moses's prayer answered? *"And the LORD descended in the cloud, and stood with him there, and proclaimed the name of the LORD. And the LORD passed by before him, and proclaimed, The LORD, The LORD God, merciful and gracious, longsuffering, and abundant in goodness and truth,"* Exodus 34:5-6.

Moses knew the character of the Lord, but it was more deeply experienced that day on the cleft of the Rock. This experience can be ours when we daily step into His light of love, mercy, and grace when we demonstrate our faithfulness by setting our affections upon Him. And it will deepen when we talk faith and of His faithfulness, never doubting His love because we have put our trust in His name.

Dear Heavenly Father, may we always be found faithful to Thee. In Jesus's Name, Amen!

FAITHFUL

And in that day shall ye say, Praise the LORD, call upon His name, declare His doings among the people, make mention that His name is exalted.
Isaiah 12:4

30

QUIET PEACE

Imagine what will happen today if we rest in *quiet peace* in the Lord.

"But they that wait upon the LORD shall renew their strength; they shall mount up with wings as eagles; they shall run, and not be weary; and they shall walk, and not faint." Isaiah 40:31

When we seek the Lord in prayer and share our hearts and our need for Him, by faith, we receive His peace, and we take possession of His sweet serenity that rules our hearts. Then waiting on the Lord becomes a joyful journey instead of a wasteful wilderness experience. When we pass through those difficult places and make Christ our daily companion, we behold His glory, and by beholding, we become changed.

The soul that faithfully waits upon the Lord and makes Him their daily companion, trusting in Him, will know by experience what it is to be renewed by His strength. They will testify that they mount up with wings as eagles; they run and do not become weary.

Did you know that God loves to hear us talk about His Son, Jesus Christ? When we share with others Jesus's merit, His righteousness, His goodness, and His faithfulness, God's smiles. He also loves it when we allow the Holy Spirit to empower us to demonstrate our faithfulness to the One who is righteous, good, and faithful. O magnify the LORD with me, and let us exalt His name together today!

FAITHFUL

O LORD, Thou art my God; I will exalt Thee, I will praise Thy name; for Thou hast done wonderful things; Thy counsels of old are faithfulness and truth. Isaiah 25:1

31

SAFE PLACE

> Imagine what will happen today if we know that *Jesus is our safe place*.

ARE YOU TELLING JESUS EVERYTHING? HAVE YOU GIVEN HIM the secrets of your heart? Are you comfortable with Him searching the innermost recesses of your soul and reading your thoughts like an open book?

"I the LORD search the heart, I try the reins, even to give every man according to his ways, and according to the fruit of his doings" Jeremiah 17:10. *"O LORD, Thou hast searched me, and known me. Thou knowest my downsitting and mine uprising, Thou understandest my thought afar off"* Psalm 139:1-2.

These scriptures prove three things, God profoundly loves us, His mercy endures, and His love is aimed directly at our hearts. Think about it... Who knows everything about us and still loves us?

God has no regret sending Christ to the cross. Christ has no regrets laying down His life so that you and I can live.

None! So, get comfortable, really comfortable with being in the presence of Christ.

Faithfully turn the pages of your life over to Him, for He has declared that He is the author and is the finisher of your faith... You are His open book... and it is His face that will be seen on the front cover once all is said and done. It will be His story that is written on every page. And the back cover will read of the many testimonies of the people that have read His story about your life and how it dramatically changed theirs.

O magnify the Lord with me, and let us magnify His name together.

Dear Heavenly Father, may we always be found faithful to Thee. In Jesus's Name, Amen!

32

THE POWER OF BROKENNESS

Imagine what will happen today if we are *broken*.

CHRIST SAID IN LUKE 4:18 THAT HE CAME TO HEAL THE brokenhearted, proclaim liberty to the captives, and open the prison to them that are bound. This wasn't the first time He spoke these words, read Isaiah 61:1-3.

Jesus also said, *"And whosoever shall fall on this stone shall be broken: but on whomsoever it shall fall, it will grind him to powder."* Matthew 21:44

How can these two truths be equally true?

Hmmm... to be broken on the Rock of Christ Jesus means to denounce self-righteousness.

Christ breaks us so that He can heal our brokenness, *"Come, and let us return unto the LORD: for He hath torn, and He will heal us; He hath smitten, and He will bind us up."* Hosea 6:1

When we allow Christ to do the breaking and rebuilding, we demonstrate our faithfulness in Him. We show Him that we rest assured that He is in the process of finishing the good work He began in us (Philippians 1:6). And His continual flow of grace supplies us with His strength, for each day, unit He finishes the work he begun in us so long ago.

> *Dear Heavenly Father, may we always be found faithful to Thee. In Jesus's Name, Amen!*

FAITHFUL

Be careful for nothing; but in every thing by prayer and supplication with thanksgiving let your requests be made known unto God.
Philippians 4:6

33

CONSTANT

> Imagine what will happen today if we know that *God is constant.*

A PERSON THAT IS CONSTANT DOES NOT CHANGE. THE WORD of God says God is love (1 John 4:7). Can you think of a circumstance, situation, occasion, or period of time when God stops loving? The Bible also says that,

God is faithful. Deuteronomy 7:9; 1 Corinthians 10:13
God is merciful. Psalm 103:8-17; Hebrews 4:16
God is gracious. Psalm 145:8-13; James 4:6
God is just. Isaiah 30:18; Deuteronomy 32:4; Romans 3:36

God is constantly faithful, merciful, gracious, and just; therefore, we need not worry nor fret. And the demonstration of our faithfulness to God is shown when we cast down anything that causes us to doubt that God is constant.
2 Corinthians 10:4-5.

34

FIRST BELIEVED

Imagine what will happen today if we remember when we *first believed*.

DO YOU REMEMBER THE FIRST TIME YOU OPENED YOUR HEART to Christ? If not, ask the Holy Spirit to refresh your memory because Christ hasn't forgotten.

"For Thou hast delivered my soul from death, mine eyes from tears, and my feet from falling. I will walk before the LORD in the land of the living. ... What shall I render unto the LORD for all His benefits toward me?" Psalm 116:8-9, 12.

Dear Heavenly Father, take me back to where I first believed. Renew my faith, restore my joy. I recommit my life to You today, for You alone deserve my loyalty, trust, and praise. Amen!

FAITHFUL

It is of the LORD'S mercies that we are not consumed, because His compassions fail not. They are new every morning: great is Thy faithfulness.
Lamentations 3:22-23

35

GOD'S COURAGE

Imagine what will happen today if we move forward *in God's courage*.

"*BE STRONG AND OF A GOOD COURAGE, FEAR NOT, NOR BE afraid of them: for the LORD thy God, He it is that doth go with thee; He will not fail thee, nor forsake thee.*" Deuteronomy 31:6.

The Scottish Christian reformer John Knox said, 'There lies he who never feared the face of man.' Why? Because by faith, he had looked upon the face of God. Mary, Queen of Scots, is reported to have said, "*I fear the prayers of John Knox more than all the assembled armies of Europe.*"

What would happen today if we feared nothing but trusted holy in Christ Jesus, moving confidently, faithfully in His purpose and will. He promises that He will go with us.... He will not fail us nor forsake us.

Listen in on the Prophet Isaiah's conversation with the Father and Son, *"I heard the voice of the Lord, saying, Whom shall I send, and who will go for us? Then said I, Here am I; send me."* Isaiah 6:8

Are you ready for it to be said of you, 'I fear no man because I have looked upon the face of God?' The Father is looking for such people. Will you be that one?

Dear Heavenly Father, may we always be found faithful to Thee. In Jesus's Name, Amen!

> My voice shalt Thou hear in the morning, O LORD; in the morning will I direct my prayer unto Thee, and will look up.
> Psalm 5:3

Are you watchful? Are you Mindful? Vigilant? Looking to see where God is leading so that you will faithfully follow.

FAITHFUL

*Have not I commanded thee?
Be strong and of a good
courage; be not afraid, neither
be thou dismayed: for the
LORD Thy God is with thee
whithersoever thou goest.
Joshua 1:9*

36

GOD'S MERCY

Imagine what will happen today if we *rest in God's mercy*.

"*BE MERCIFUL UNTO ME, O GOD, BE MERCIFUL UNTO ME: FOR my soul trusteth in Thee: yea, in the shadow of Thy wings will I make my refuge, until these calamities be overpast.*" Psalm 57:1

Life is interesting with all of its twists and turns. Yet God is merciful.

And He hears our calls for help. But what happens when things don't turn out the way we planned. When circumstances appear to take us far from where we planned to be.

When David was a young boy, the Prophet Samuel anointed him to be the next king of Israel. Yet here he is, running for his life. Had God changed His mind? What was taking so long for God to fulfill His word?

No, God had not changed His mind. He was teaching David how to be faithful in times of test and trial.

He learned lessons of mercy and what it meant to hide in the shadow of God's wings.

When God has another plan to fulfill His will, just say yes. Remain faithful because He knows what's best. Rest in His sovereign will until it's all comes to pass.

Hallelujah, Hallelujah and Amen!

Dear Heavenly Father, may we always be found faithful to Thee. In Jesus's Name, Amen!

> Enter into His gates with thanksgiving, and into His courts with praise: be thankful unto Him, and bless His name. For the LORD is good; His mercy is everlasting; and His truth endureth to all generations.
> Psalm 100:4-5

37

REJOICING

Imagine what will happen if we face today *rejoicing*.

"BELOVED, THINK IT NOT STRANGE CONCERNING THE FIERY trial which is to try you, as though some strange thing happened unto you: But rejoice, inasmuch as ye are partakers of Christ's sufferings; that, when His glory shall be revealed, ye may be glad also with exceeding joy." 1 Peter 4:12–13

Wow! The Christian journey is nothing to take likely or for granted. The Apostle Peter did not say, concerning the fiery trial, that '*might*' try you, but 'which *is to try you*, as something strange happening to you.

We accept it. Count on it. Look for it. Because the fiery trial, which is to try (our faith), will continue to happen until Jesus comes.

The good news is, Jesus measures each trial so that we are not given more than we can carry. And He doesn't leave us alone in the trial.

When it seems the darkest of the night... Our faithfulness is severely tested, He is the nearest to us. And with the heart/mind of faith, we know this, and we experience His peace beyond our understanding.

Then we start emerging from these fiery trials with a renewed purpose and determination to live for Christ. To share the good news of salvation and His soon return. Our faith becomes faithful to the end. And we desire nothing more than to bring glory and honor to Jesus.

Hallelujah, Hallelujah and Amen!

Dear Heavenly Father, may we always be found faithful to Thee. In Jesus's Name, Amen!

FAITHFUL

*My voice shalt Thou hear in the
morning, O LORD; in the
morning will I direct my
prayer unto Thee,
and will look up.
Psalm 5:3*

38

GOD'S MIND

Imagine what will happen today if we know we are on God's mind.

DAVID SAID TO THE LORD, *"HOW PRECIOUS ALSO ARE THY thoughts unto me, O God! how great is the sum of them! If I should count them, they are more in number than the sand: when I awake, I am still with Thee."* Psalm 139:17–18

Imagine what would happen if we accepted the truth that God loves us. He cares for and about us. How precious are His thoughts, His tender loving thoughts toward us?

He sees our true hearts/mind condition before Him, and His thoughts are still precious towards us, and they are as numerous as the sand. Wow...

The truth, when accepted in the heart, will make us free. And we can be free all the time when we know that the power of God always attends to the truth found in His word. Therefore, take Him at His word when He said His thoughts toward us are precious.

Do you believe it? If not, what lie is holding you back from abiding in the truth? Determine to be free of that lie that holds you back and live the abundant life God has for you today.

Hallelujah, Hallelujah and Amen.

Dear Heavenly Father, may we always be found faithful to Thee. In Jesus's Name, Amen!

> For I know the thoughts that I think toward you, saith the LORD, thoughts of peace, and not of evil, to give you an expected end. Then shall ye call upon Me, and ye shall go and pray unto Me, and I will hearken unto you. And ye shall seek Me, and find Me, when ye shall search for Me with all your heart.
> Jeremiah 29:11-13

39

GOD IS BIG ENOUGH

Imagine what will happen today if we know that God is big enough.

SOMETIMES WE QUESTION IF GOD IS BIG ENOUGH TO MEET our needs. Sometimes we wonder if God sees us or if He take an interest in what concerns us. *"Am I a God at hand, saith the LORD, and not a God afar off? Can any hide himself in secret places that I shall not see him? saith the LORD. Do not I fill heaven and earth? saith the LORD."* Jeremiah 23:23–24

When we see God correctly, our anxious hearts and troubled thoughts will disappear. How is this possible? The same God that spoke and the world was created is the same God we bring our anxious hearts and troubled thoughts to.

Ask yourself… What is too hard for God? Nothing! Absolutely nothing. Read the truth about Him. Believe the truth about Him. Then experience how big and vast He is. He declares Himself to fill not just heaven but the earth as well.

Lord, fill us with Your love, courage, power, and peace to see and know and experience You today.

You declare your faithfulness when you say; Lord God, You are big enough for anything I will face today.
Hallelujah, Hallelujah, and Amen!

Dear Heavenly Father, may we always be found faithful to Thee. In Jesus's Name, Amen!

> Thus saith the LORD the maker thereof, the LORD that formed it, to establish it; the LORD is His name; Call unto Me, and I will answer thee, and shew thee great and mighty things, which thou knowest not.
> Jeremiah 33:2-3

FAITHFUL

*Enter into His gates with
thanksgiving, and into His
courts with praise: be thankful
unto Him, and bless His name.
For the LORD is good; His
mercy is everlasting; and His
truth endureth to
all generations.
Psalm 100:4-5*

40

EVEN THIS...

Imagine what will happen today if we give to God *even this...*

FOR MY CLOSING THOUGHTS, I WILL SHARE AN EXPERIENCE I had with the Lord that changed my life. It was during a time of prayer and deep searching, wanting nothing to stand between my Lord and me. In many ways, it was the beginning of my need to be faithful to Him. What I learned was Jesus has done it all. There is no need for additional evidence of His faithfulness. It's all there. When I accepted that, opening up the hidden places in my life to Jesus became as natural as breathing. I knew then; it was my honor and privilege to prove to Him that He could be trusted. I knew this task would be impossible without my complete surrender to the Holy Spirit. So it is my daily prayer that He shows me ways to display my love, loyalty, and faithfulness to the One who loves me so much.

As I descend the stairs, Jesus walks close behind me. I'm leading Him through a long passageway to a closed, sealed room called pain.

It's very dark, but strangely enough, I can see my way. Maybe it's the light that naturally shines from Jesus that gives me comfort and lights my path.

I want to show Him this room. I've never thought to take Him there before. Today, I'm not afraid to show Him this room.

Finally, we're at the bottom of the stairs. The room is just a few steps away. I wonder if it's locked... Did I remember to bring the key? I check my pockets. No key. I reach to open the door, it doesn't open, but it's not locked. That's strange. I tug on it; now I have to put both hands on the doorknob and pull hard. It opens, but the years have caused it to swell from the dampness. It scarps against the floor, but I'm determined to get this door opened.

I slip through the small opening, and once on the other side, I push hard to make room for Jesus to come through it. Finally, the door is open.

It's a dark place. No windows. One way in... One way out... No lights. It smells old, moldy... Cobwebs have overtaken the place.

I haven't been here in years, yet it feels strangely familiar.

I step aside and invite Jesus to come in; I say, 'Come,' and motion with my hand, 'Come.' He walks through the door, and I say to Him... this is it...

He looks around taking it all in. He turns to me and says, with the slightest of smile... *Even this*...

I bury my face in His side and weep, and He puts His arms around me. Yes... *Even this* He can heal. *Even this* He can redeem. *Even this* He can restore. *Even in this* I can prove myself faithful to God.

And He reminds me.... that His love, mercy and grace is deeper than any pain or experience I have to show Him. He promises to teach me how to be faithful to Him and that He will finish the work He has begun in me.

We climb the stairs arm and arm. This room I once called pain is no longer mine for I have laid it at the foot of the cross. It no longer holds me captive to my past.

When I think of this room now, it has a new name. Victory!

Jesus kept His promise, now He empowers me to keep mine. Hallelujah! Hallelujah! Amen!

Thank you for coming on this short journey with me. Your company has meant a lot. I hope and pray that you were blessed by reading glimpses of my journey with God. It's far from over. Let us keep praying for each other and for Jesus soon return. Let Him find us *Faithful to the End*!

> *Dear Heavenly Father, may we always be found faithful to Thee. In Jesus's Name, Amen!*

God has been good, merciful, and gracious to us; He gave us His Son. It will take eternity to find the words that adequately offer Him the praise due to Him. Yet, we can begin today by asking the Holy Spirit to teach us how to demonstrate our faithfulness, appreciation, and allegiance to the One who gave us all.

FAITHFUL

*But I will sing of Thy power;
yea, I will sing aloud of Thy
mercy in the morning: for Thou
hast been my defence and
refuge in the day of my trouble.
Unto Thee, O my strength, will
I sing: for God is my defence,
and the God of my mercy.*
Psalm 59:16–17

www.ingramcontent.com/pod-product-compliance
Lightning Source LLC
Chambersburg PA
CBHW060835050426
42453CB00008B/699